"I don't like being happy all the time.
It makes me feel tired."
Julia - age 4

"Happy Hannah *and the* Feeling Friends *teach young kids how to deal with their emotions by applying some principles of mindfulness. This book collection is a great tool for teachers and parents."*

    Dr. Daniel Cordovani Physician, Educator

"What a great educational tool that is fun for kids and parents alike! Expressing both negative and positive feelings allows us to live emotionally full lives. It's refreshing to read a book that helps children, parents and educators express and embrace the feelings we all have."

    Katie McBean, Occupational Therapist Practicing in Paediatrics

"Thank you, Colleen, for this wonderful educational book. You are covering areas that most schools are lacking. Kids don't get taught anywhere else how to express their own feelings or how to deal with their friends, parents and mentors. This book is amazing! It also illustrates techniques of meditation and mindfulness packaged in a fun story for little kids. Fantastic educational tool for today's families!"

    Dr. Jussi Eerikäinen, International Bestselling Author, Cardiologist, Mathematician

"I love Hannah and I think every child should get to know Hannah and learn from her how to express their feelings with others. Thank you Hannah."

    Joanna Durkin, CEO Academy of International Youth Education

Published by Hasmark Publishing
http://www.hasmarkpublishing.com

Copyright© 2017 by Colleen Aynn
First Edition, 2017

No part of this book may be reproduced or transmitted in any form or by any means, electronic or mechanical, including photocopying, recording or by any information storage and retrieval system, without written permission from the author, except for the inclusion of brief quotations in a review.

Disclaimer

This book is designed to provide entertainment to readers and is sold purely for entertainment purposes. This is a work of fiction. Characters, names, places, events, incidents and circumstances are a product of the author's imagination and are used fictitiously. Any resemblance to actual persons, living or dead, business establishments, companies or locales is entirely coincidental and is not intended by the author.

The publisher does not have control over and does not assume responsibility for the author or third party websites. Neither the publisher nor the individual author(s) shall be liable for any physical, psychological, emotional, financial, or commercial damages, including, but not limited to special, incidental, consequential, or other damages.

Permission should be addressed in writing to Colleen Aynn at feelingfriendsfeedback@gmail.com

Illustrator: MATRIX Media Solutions (P) Ltd.
www.matrixnmedia.com

Cover Designer: Colleen Aynn

Layout: Anne Karklins
annekarklins@gmail.com

ISBN 13: 978-1-988071-63-3
ISBN 10: 1988071631

HAPPY HANNAH

by
Colleen Aynn

Introduction

Happy is a great feeling. We all love it.

It's wonderful to feel, and for most of us the ultimate goal of our lives. "I just want to be happy."

But what does that mean? What does it look like?

I don't think we're all that sure.

Many of us walk around with great big smiles on our faces, even when we're feeling more like crying or punching someone in the face.

Why are we doing that???

Is it just too scary to acknowledge that we're not where we want to be? We're not as picture perfect as our profiles claim to be?

We've opened up giant windows into our lives but closed off access to the inner parts of us that need to be seen the most.

Do other people's lives just look so good that we plaster our hearts and paste on a perfect smile to fit in? To distract? To hide?

Big smiles, positive thinking and affirmations are wonderful and work beautifully to help us create the lives of our dreams, but not if they're slapped on top of a pile of misery and hurt, sadness and anger.

We can't change what we don't acknowledge.

The first step to creating a life that makes us truly happy is to acknowledge that we're currently NOT happy.

We need to figure out the areas of our lives where we'd like to make a change, a shift.

And that is scary work. Taking off the mask is terrifying.

But it's the most liberating thing we can ever do – for ourselves and our families.

Once we've done that, we can take steps towards a life that actually feels good, not just one that looks good and shiny.

Everyone wins when we live a life that's filled and overflowing with joy.

Take a risk. Take it off.

And when you see someone else peeling back the layers, lend your support. It's scary work, but it's the only way to wake up each and every morning truly happy, with a deep smile in our soul.

C xo

*For every woman who's holding it together,
making it happen & gettin' 'er done.*

*We see you.
We honour you.
We thank you.
You are enough.
More than enough.
Just as you are.
Today.*

*Exhale.
Be you.
Fully you.*

We love you.

C xo

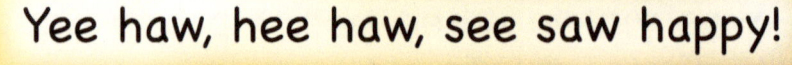
Yee haw, hee haw, see saw happy!

She smiled when her friends whispered rough, nasty words.

She smiled bright even if her feelings were hurt.

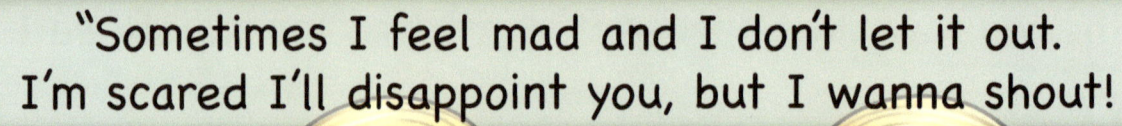

"Sometimes I feel mad and I don't let it out.
I'm scared I'll disappoint you, but I wanna shout!

I want to cry and get scared and feel small.
Get nervous, excited and be me, above all!"

Hannah took a breath and looked into each face,
then she felt a smile rise from a deep inside place.

"Up until now I've shown only one side
but there's so much more to me deep down inside."

About the Author

Colleen is the #1 International Bestselling Author of *Sad Sally*, the first of the Feeling Friends. Having experienced firsthand the healing power of expression, she designed the *Feeling Friends* series to empower children and adults to deal with and express their emotions in positive, healthy ways.

Colleen is also a Professional Speaker Coach & Creator of The EPIC System. For over 30 years she spent her life on stages around the globe as a Professional Actress, Singer and Director. Colleen has now taken this knowledge and experience and broken it down into easy, implementable steps, inspiring people to boldly express themselves and bring their unique voices to the world. Her interactive workshops and online courses teach others how to communicate their message with influence and confidence both on stage and in front of the camera. Come on over to colleenaynn.com and say hi!

Colleen still loves to get up on stage and belt out a tune, and these days she's most often joined by her awesome husband, Bruno and little firecracker, Emilia. Colleen lives in Burlington, Ontario.

"Feeling Friends"

are excited to introduce you to their new friends

The Literary Fairies

TLF is a cool place where you can find out
how YOU could become a published author or
how to help grant a literary wish.
Have an adult visit TLF website for more details about
what we do and how you can help, and also get your
FREE colouring pages and "fill-in-the-blank story"

http://theliteraryfairies.com/free-for-kids/

Join *Sad Sally*, *Mad Michael*, *Nervous Nelly* and *Happy Hannah* and all their friends as they navigate through big, emotional days with the help of some wise animal friends.

Feeling Friends help parents and kids alike, deal with and express their feelings in constructive, healthy ways.

For more tools, tips and tricks or to order this magnificent series visit
feelingfriendsbooks.com
for your BONUS gifts today!

Sad Sally

Happy Hannah

Nervous Nelly

Mad Michael

www.ingramcontent.com/pod-product-compliance
Lightning Source LLC
Chambersburg PA
CBHW041537040426
42446CB00002B/126